Converse

The

F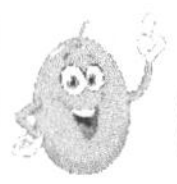ck

A vulgar adult coloring book

By

S.B. Nozaz

ATTENTION
WHORE

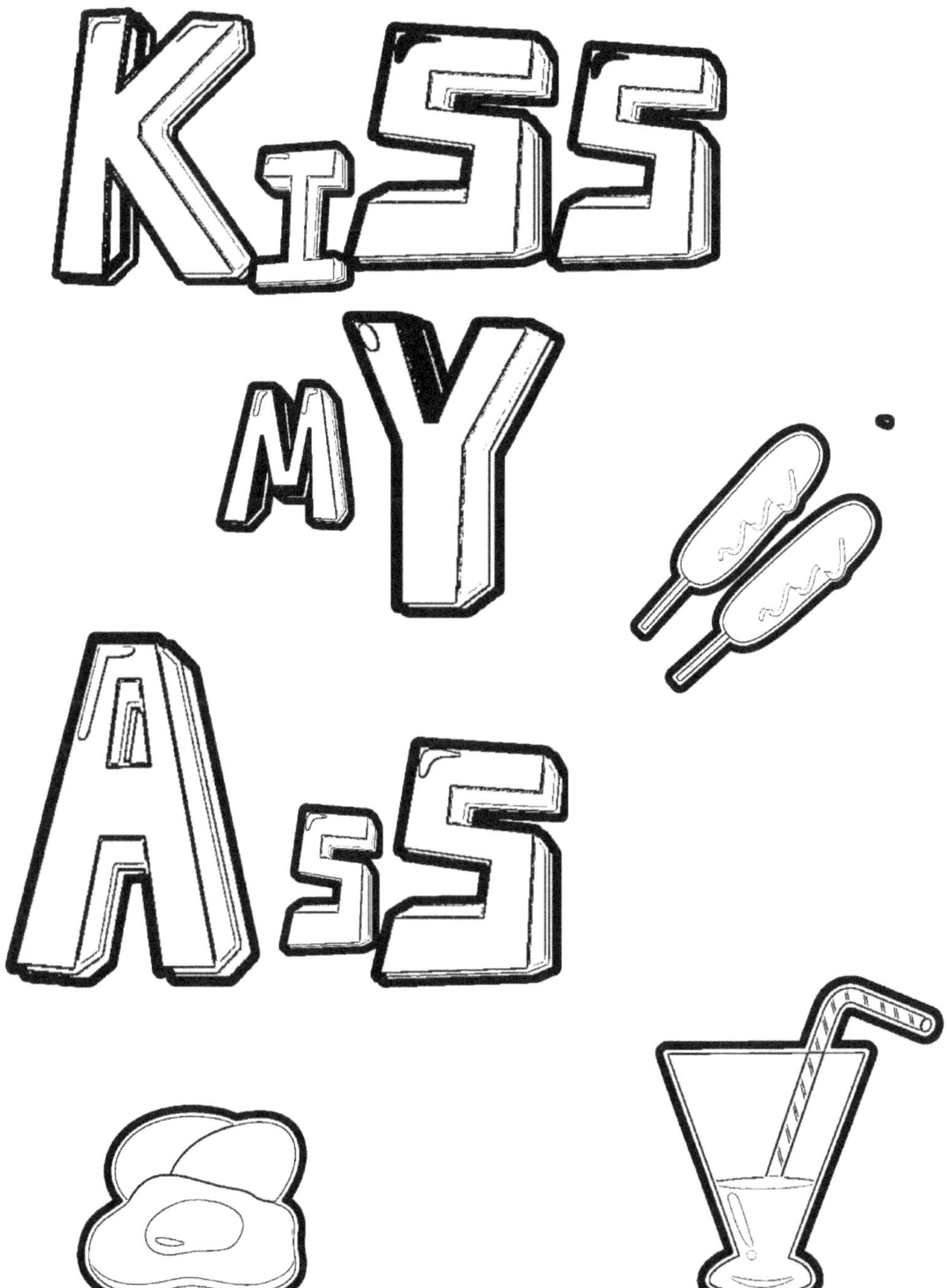
KiSS
mY
AsS

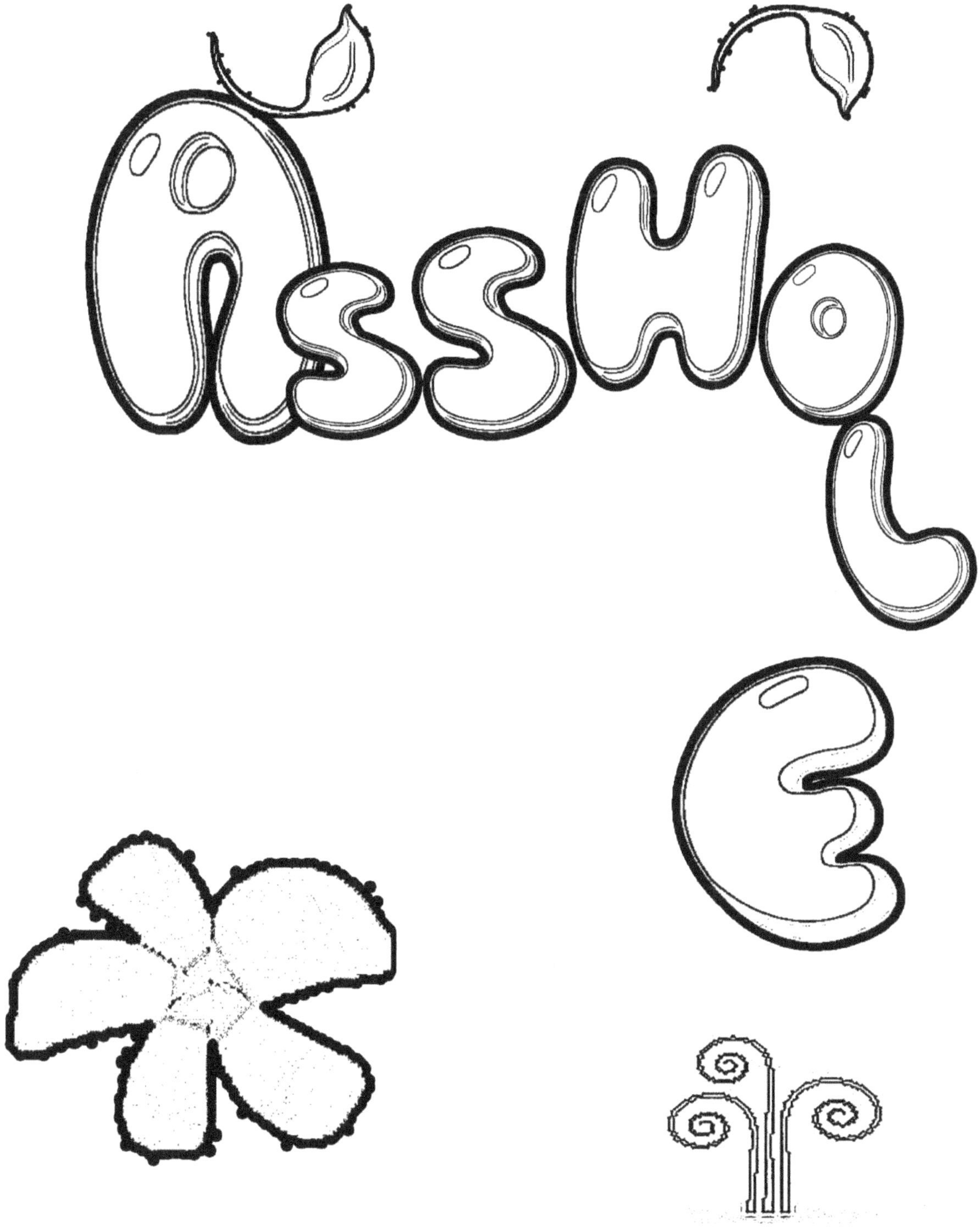
AssHole

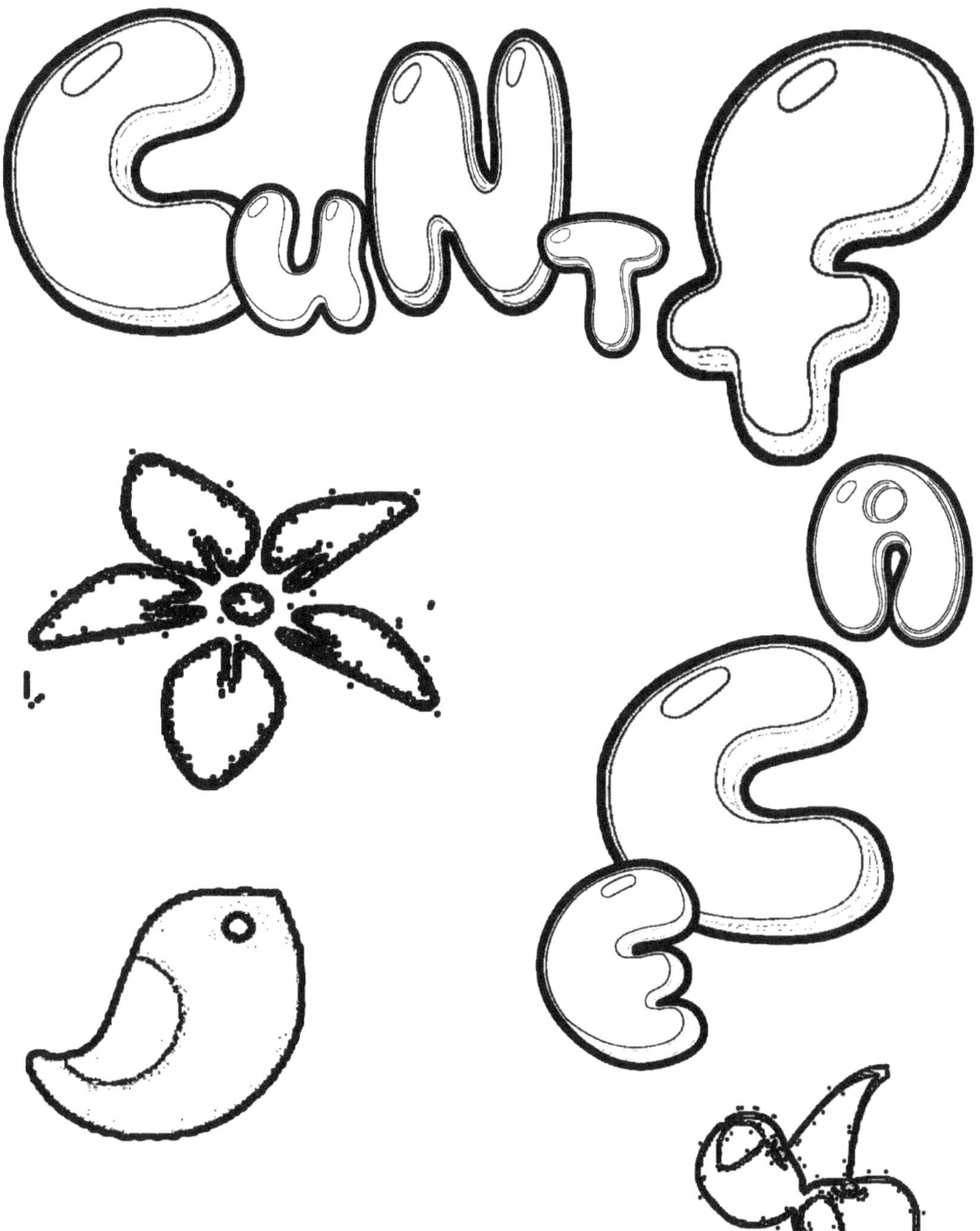
CuNt faCe

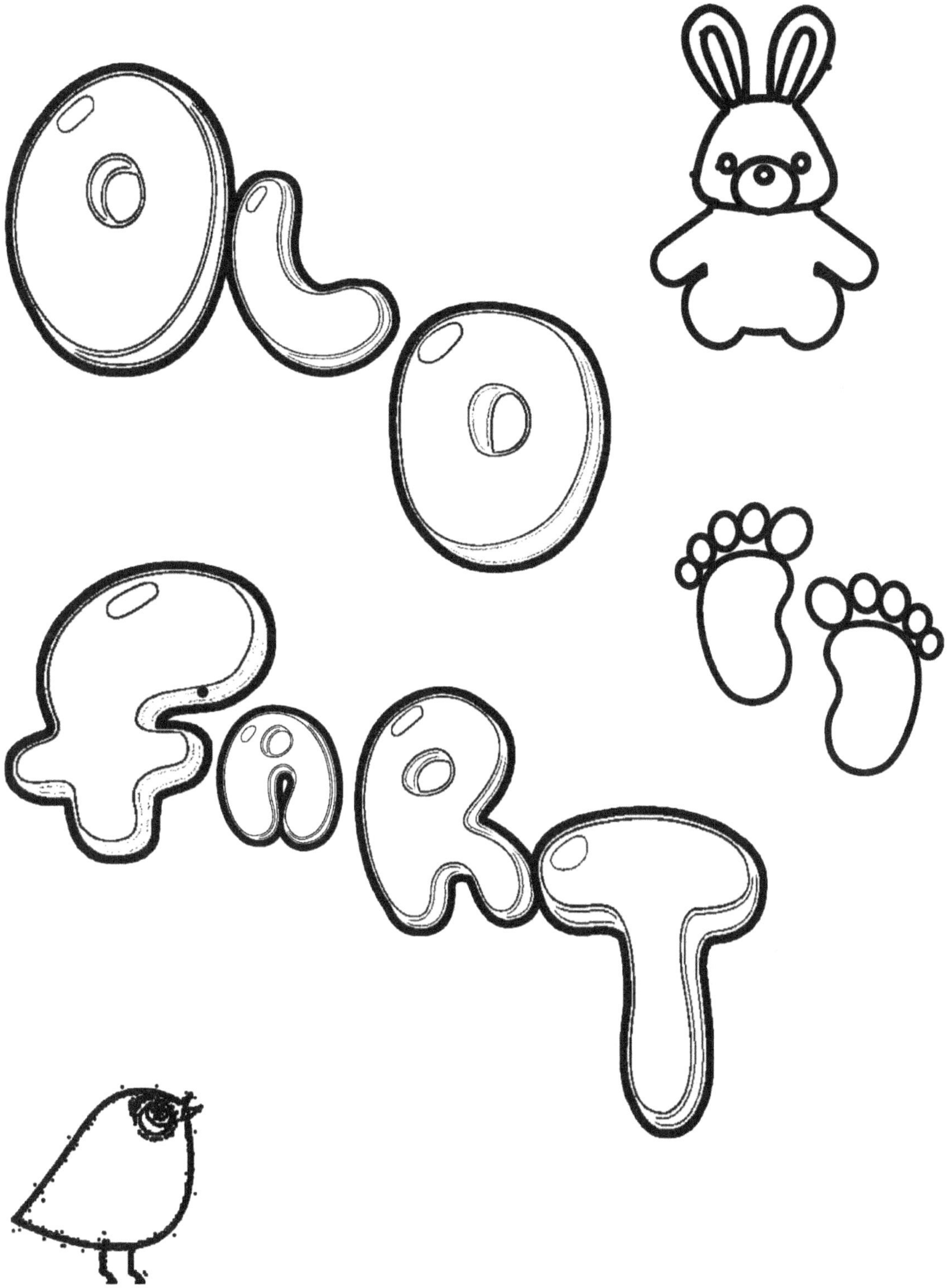
OLD
FART

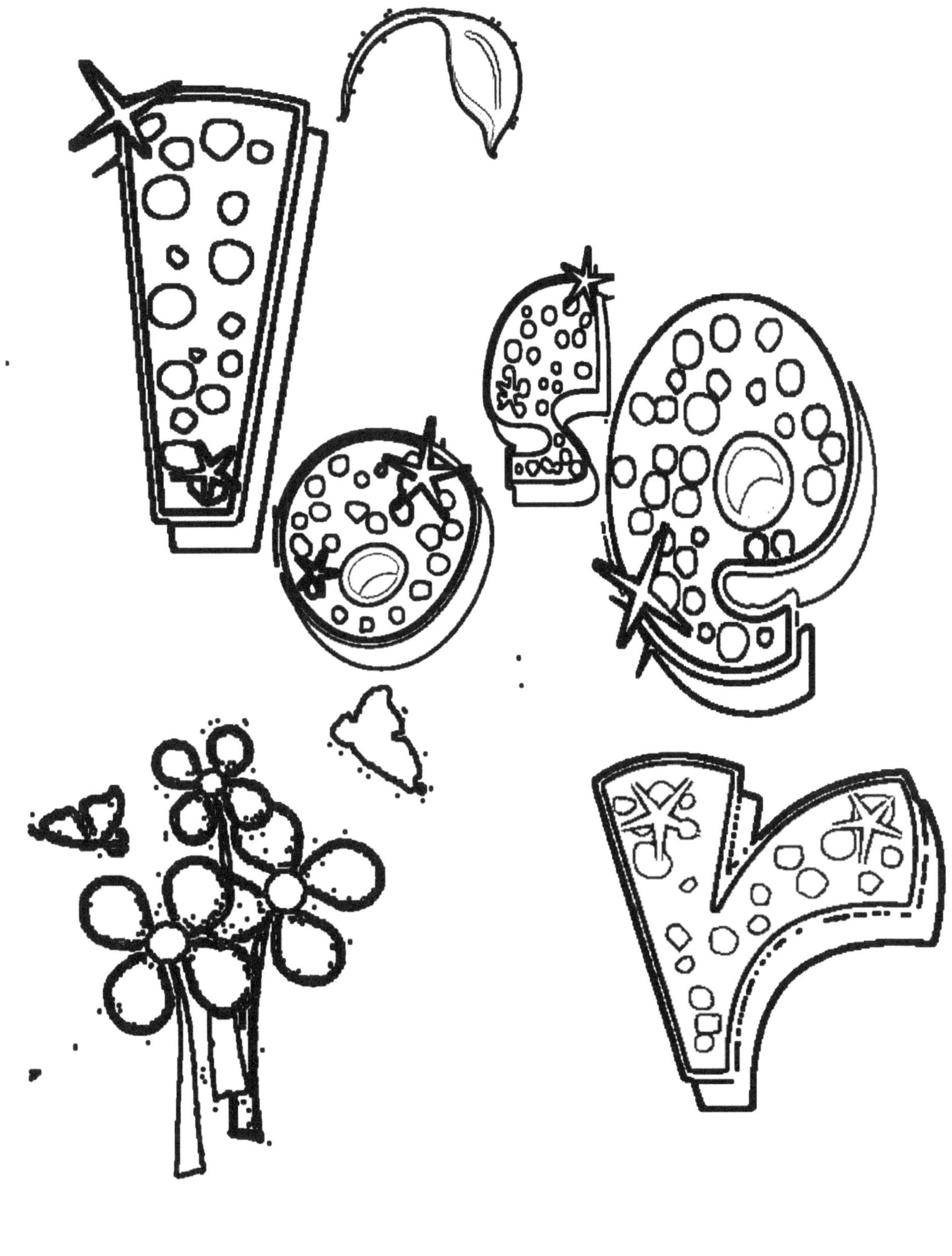

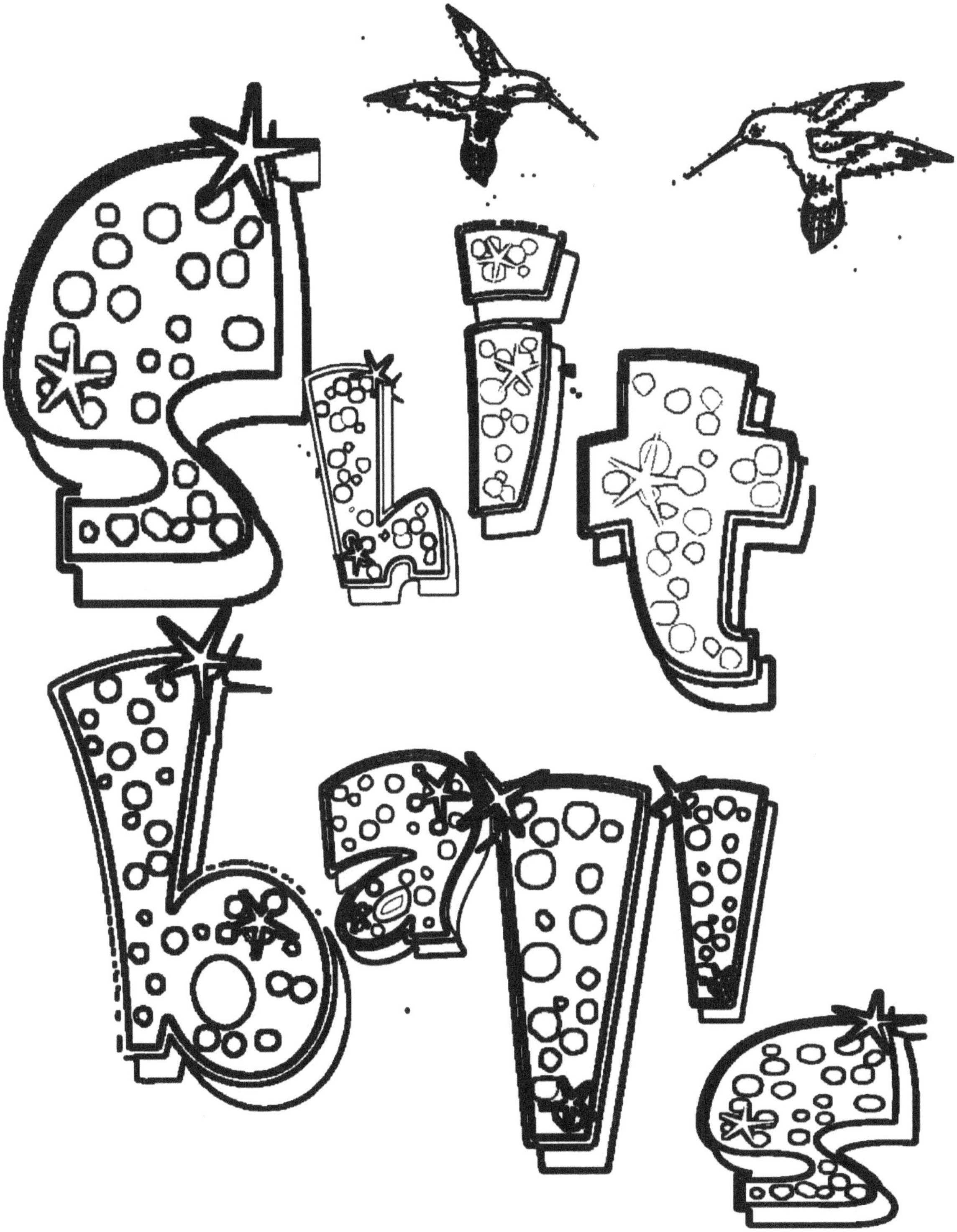

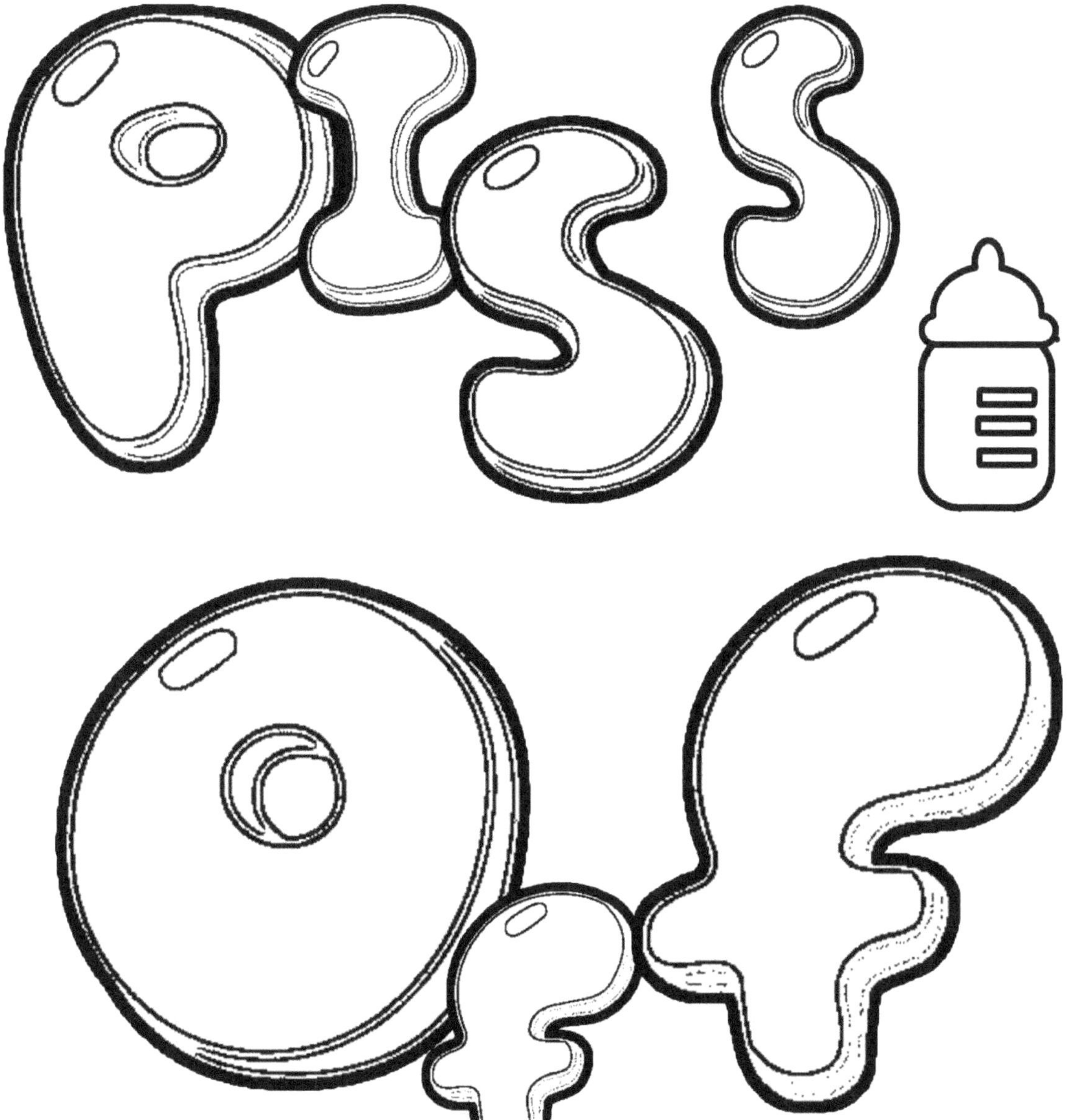
Piss
Off

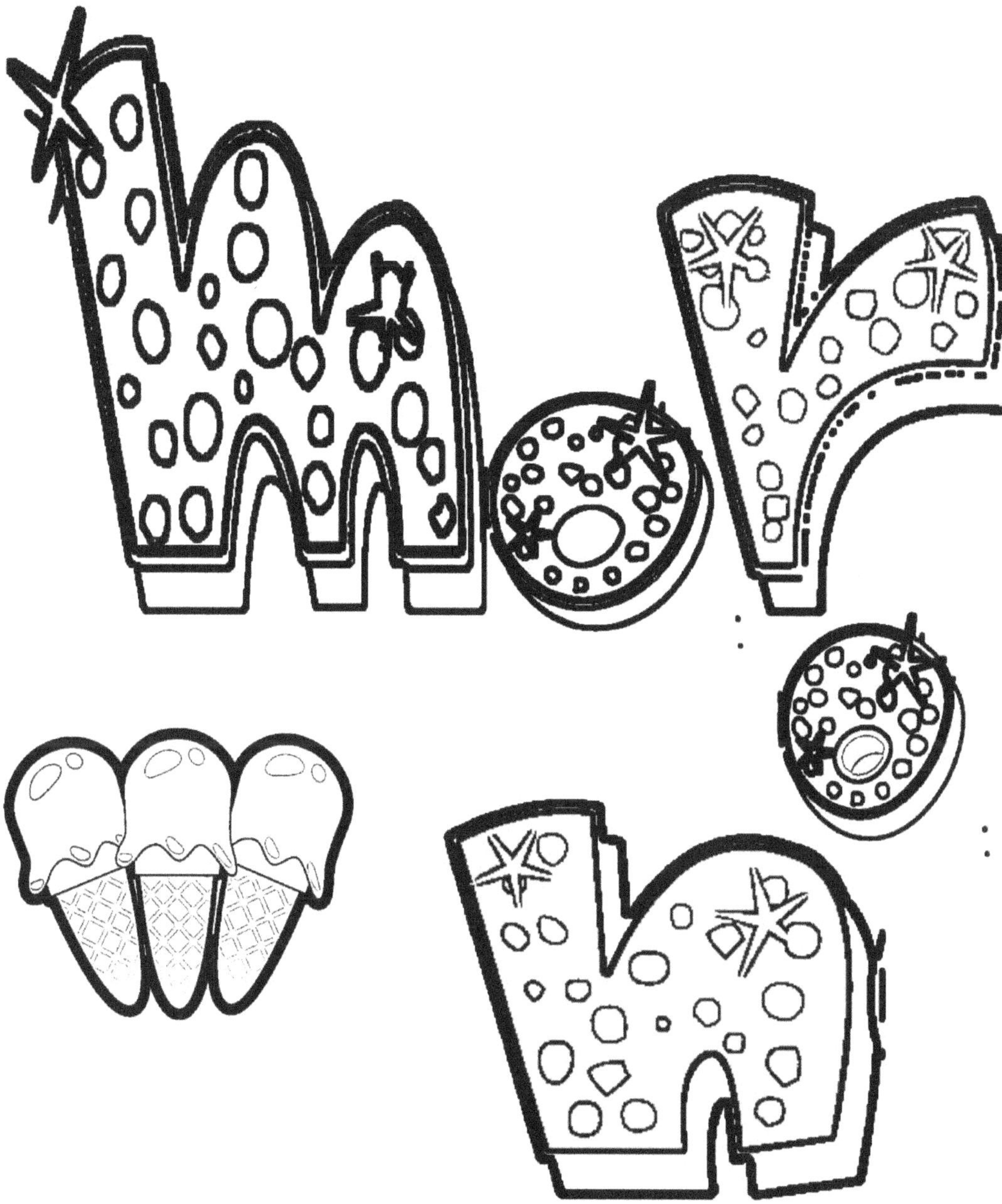
Mor
on

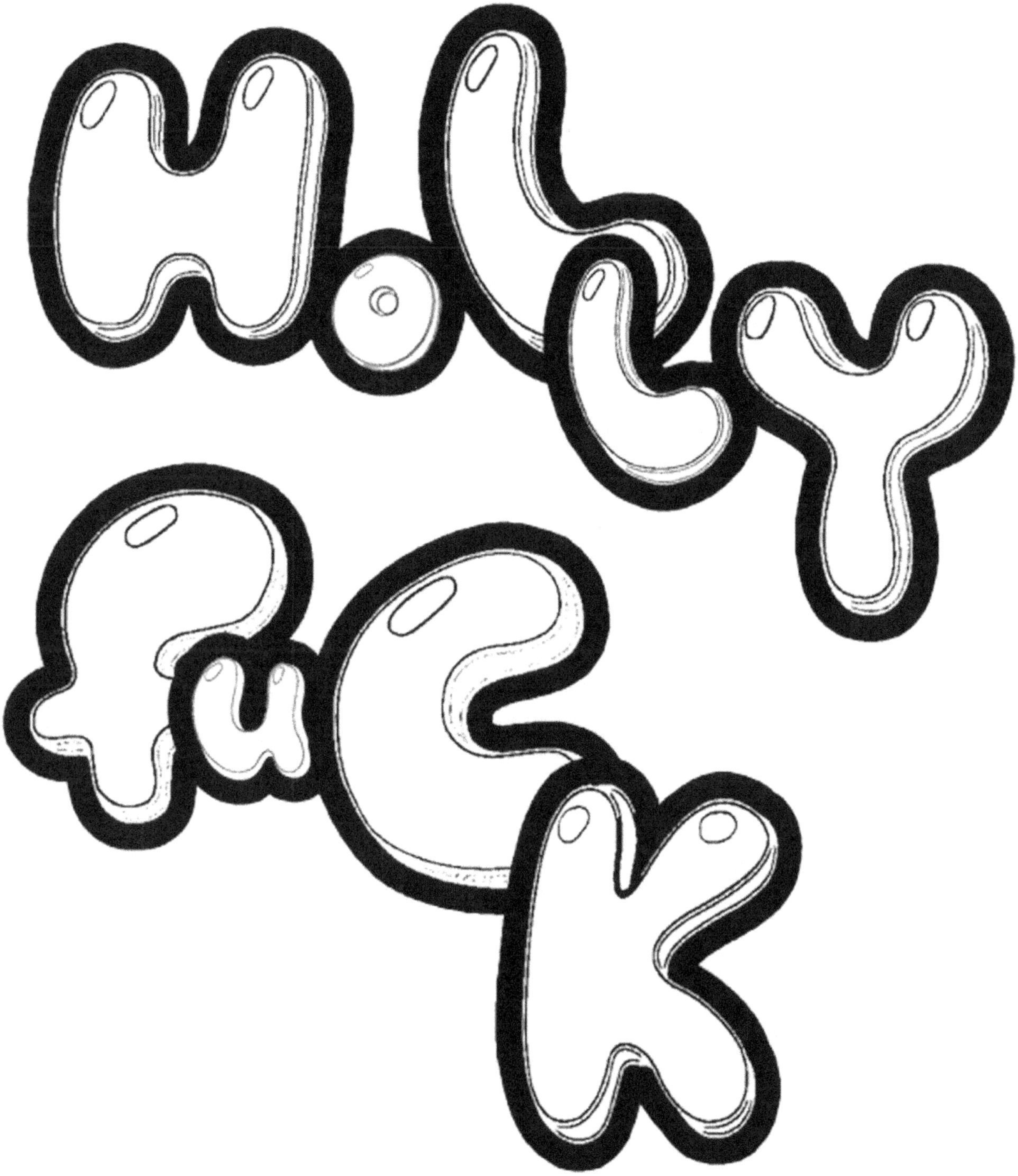
HOLY
FUCK

Ugly big shoes

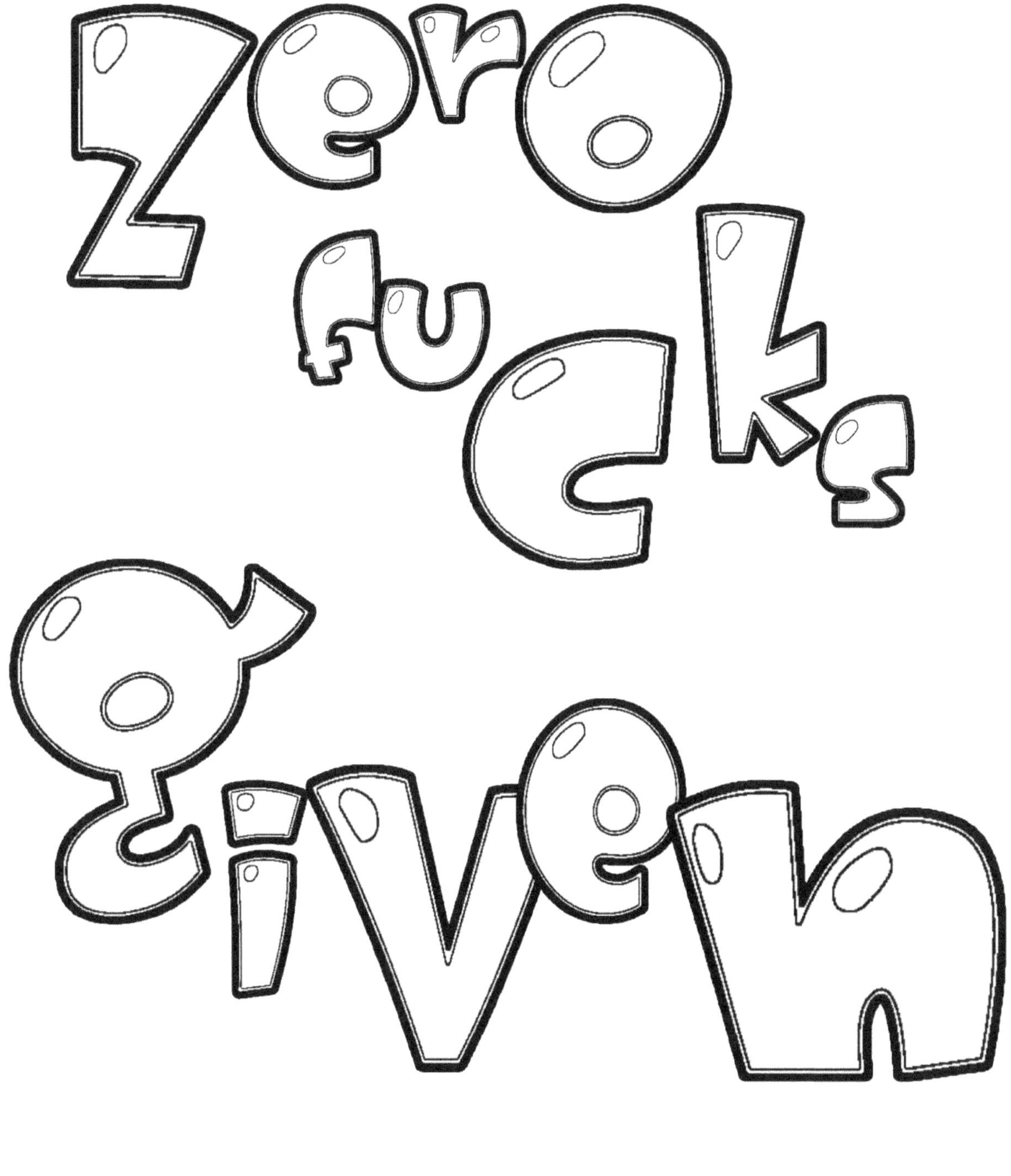
zero fucks given

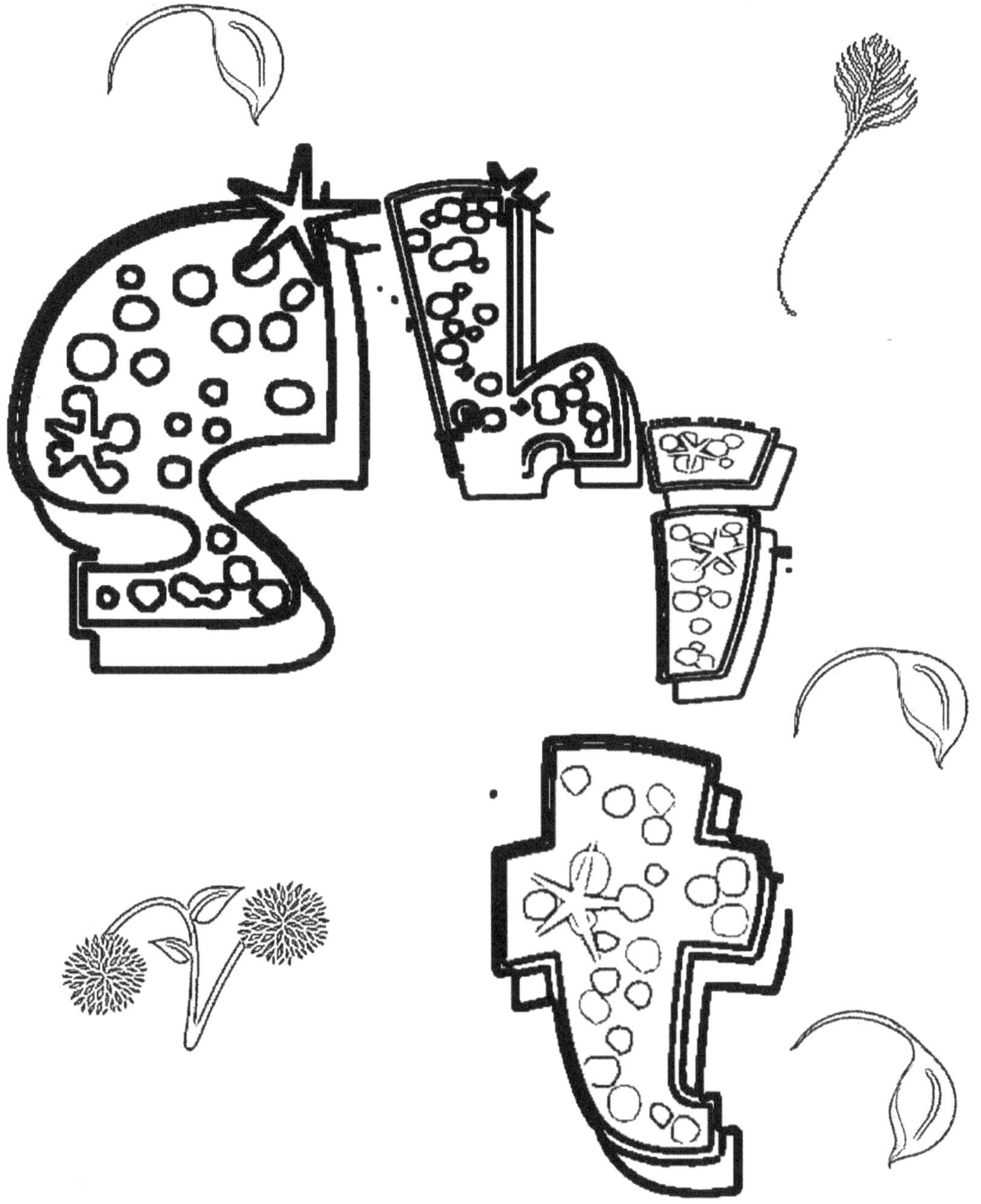
Shit

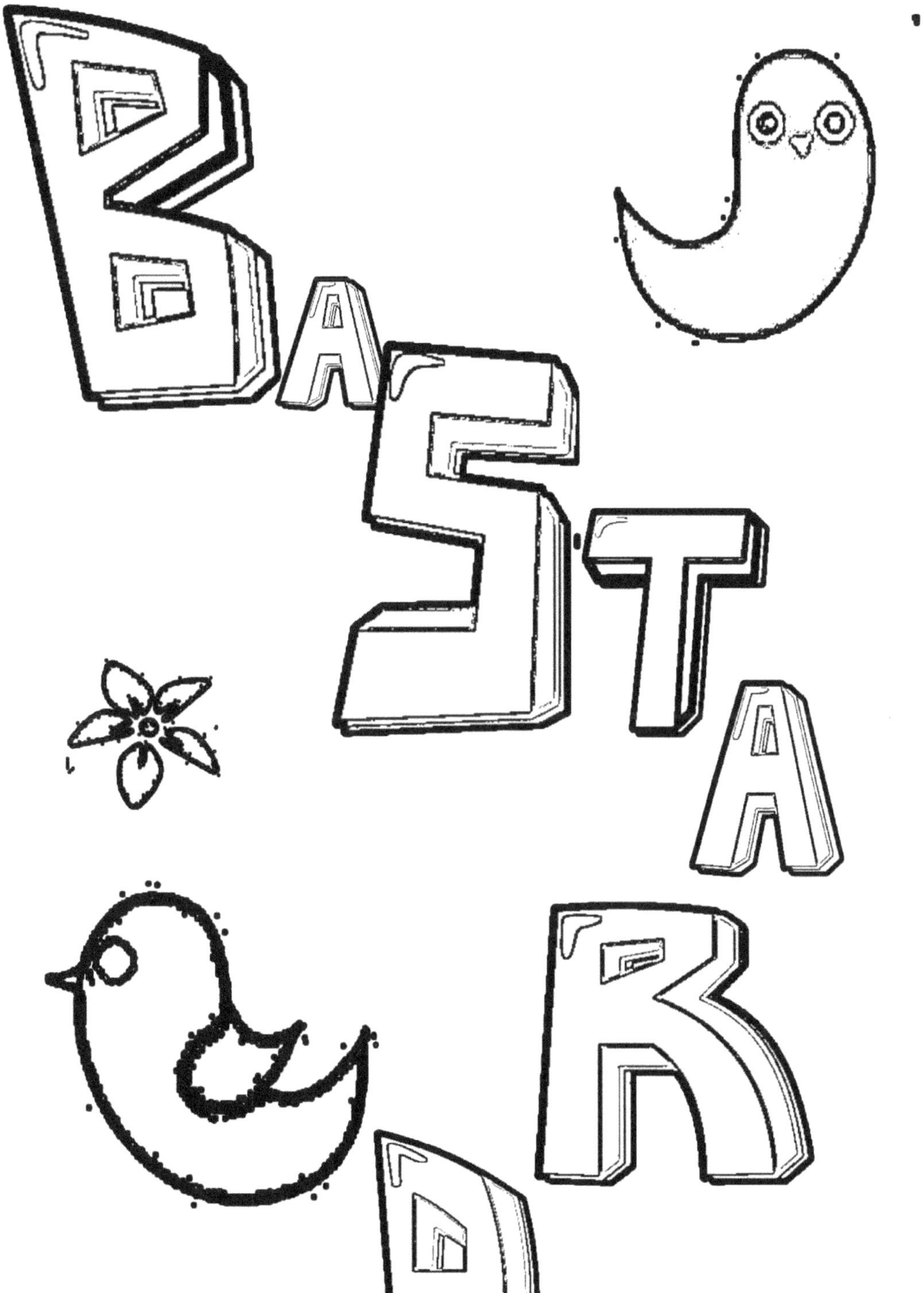
BASTARD

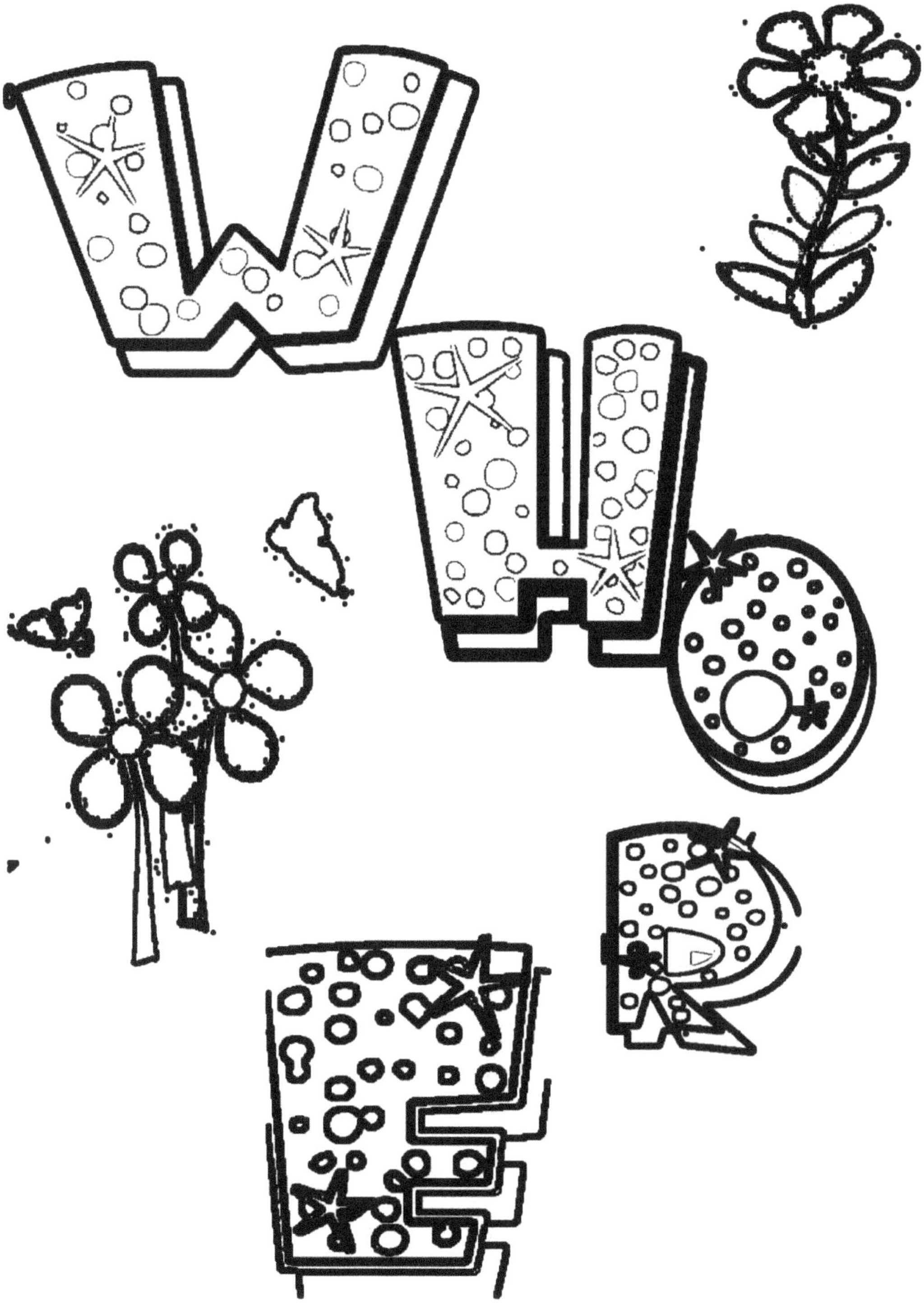
WHORE

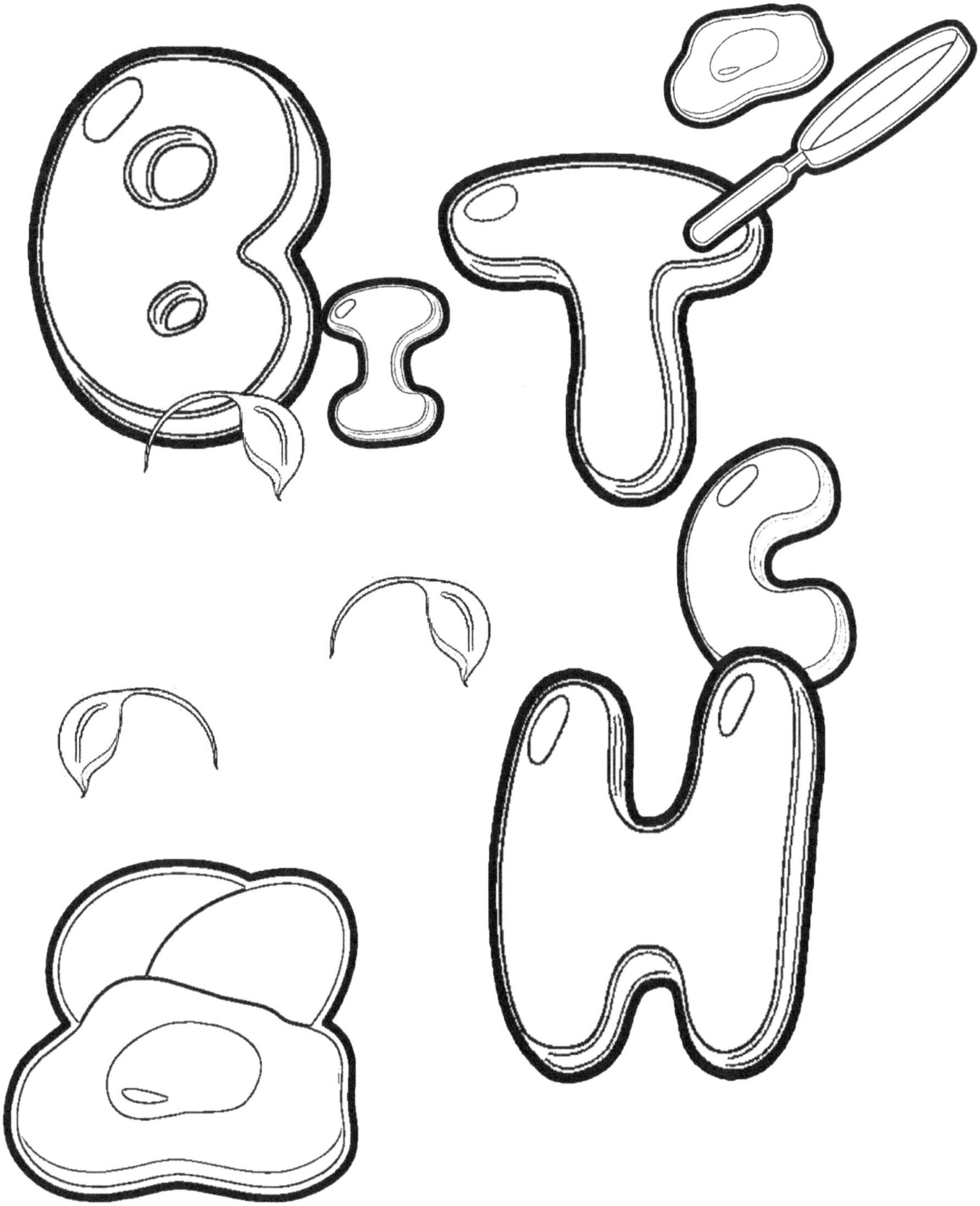

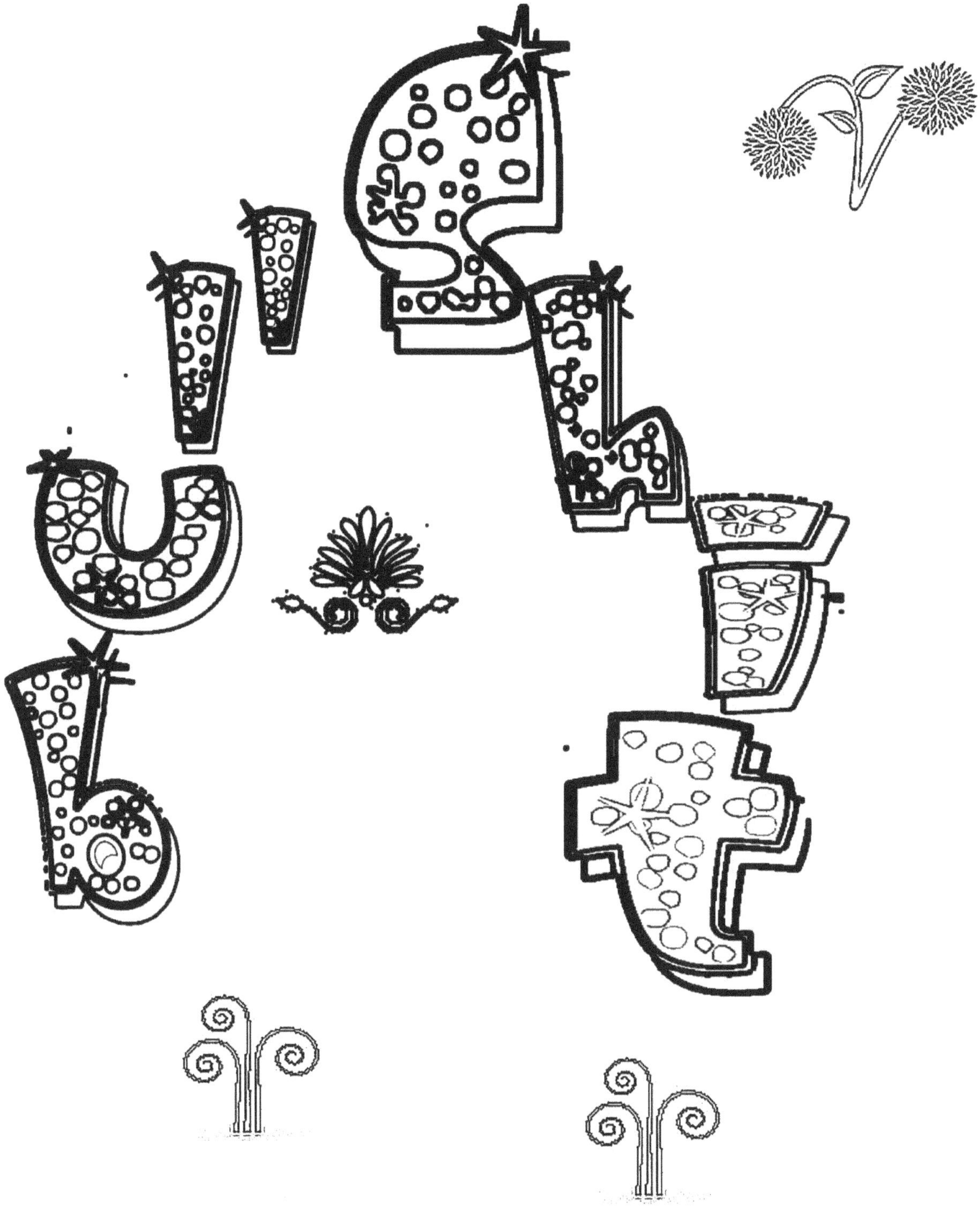
bullshit

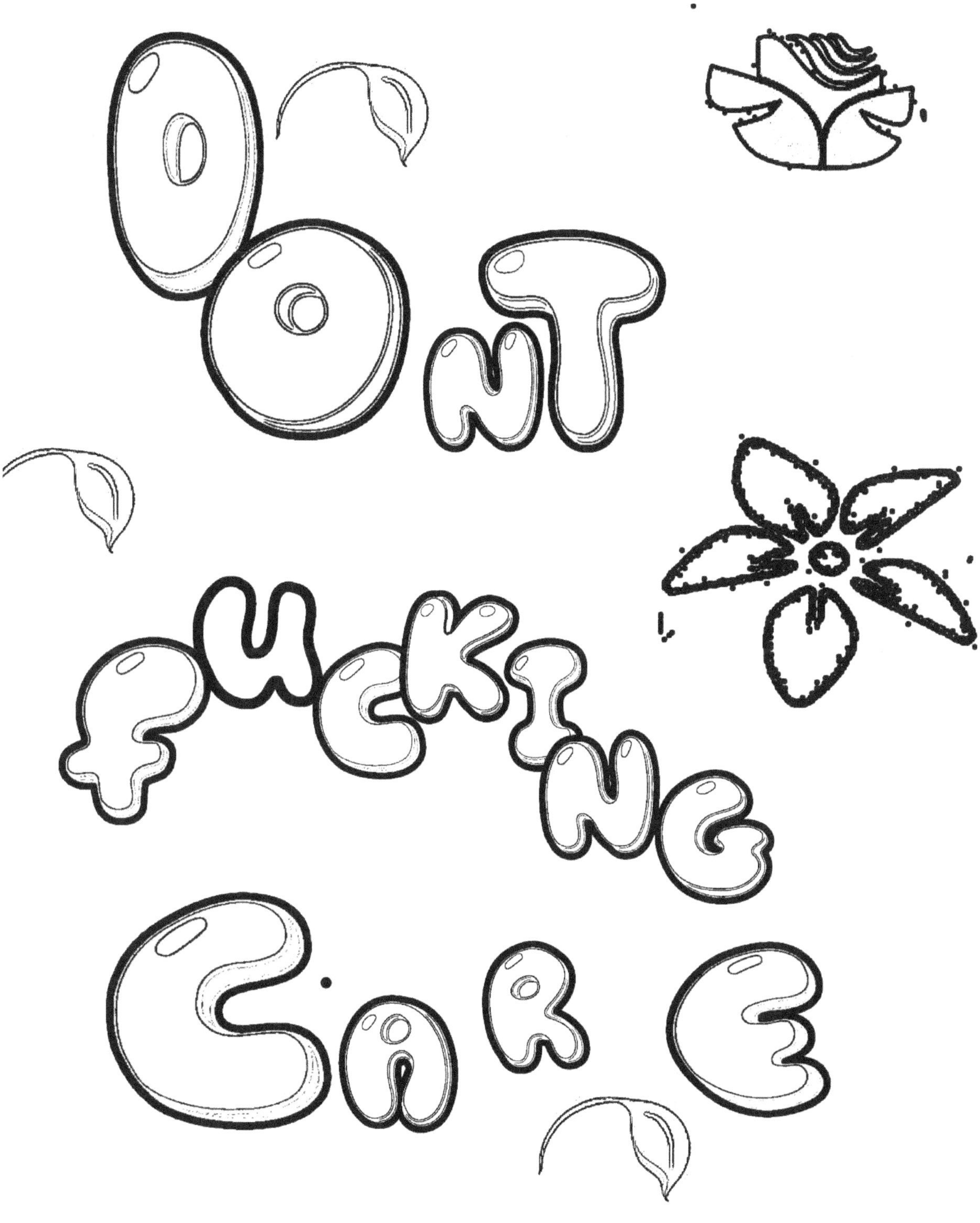
DONT
FUCKING
CARE

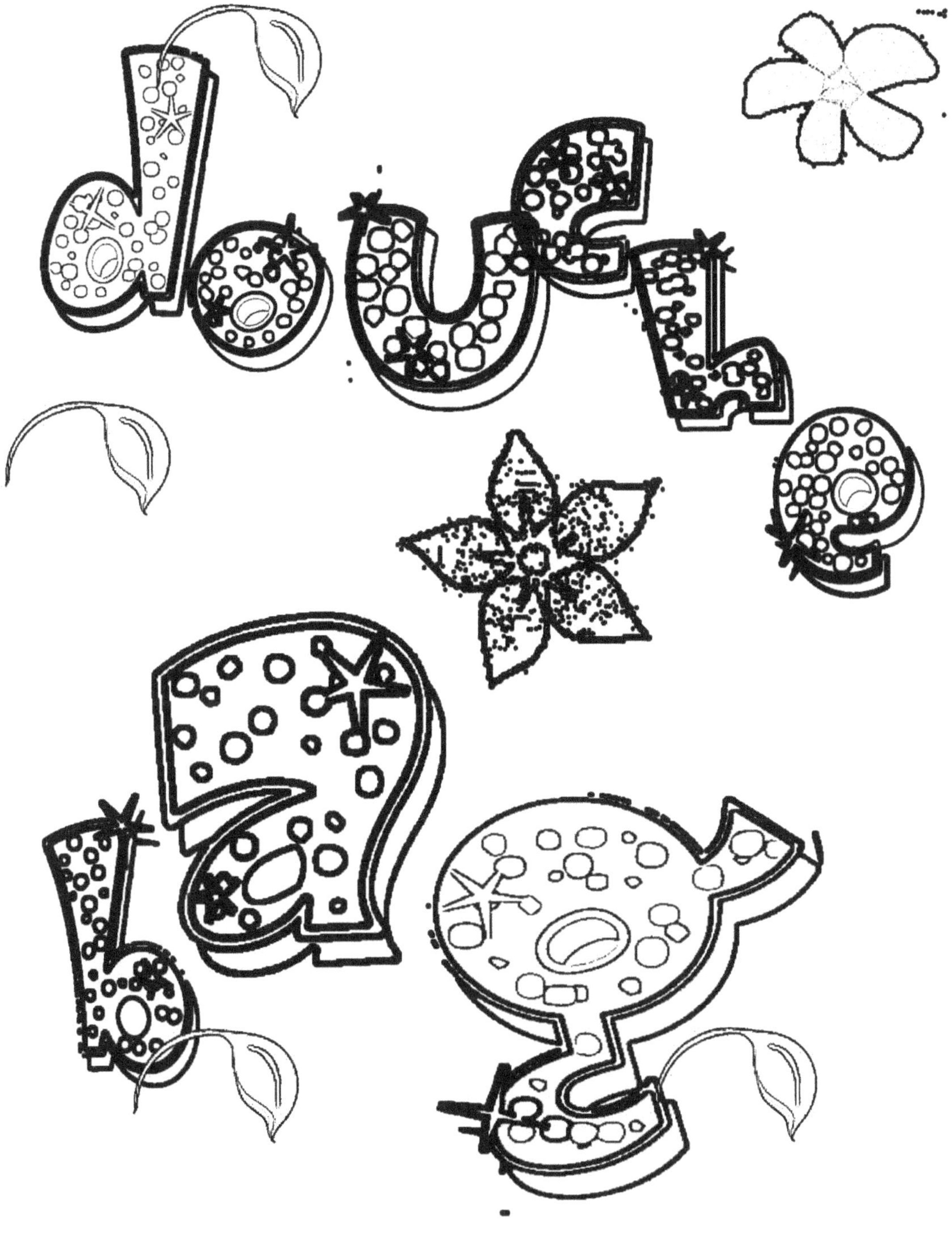

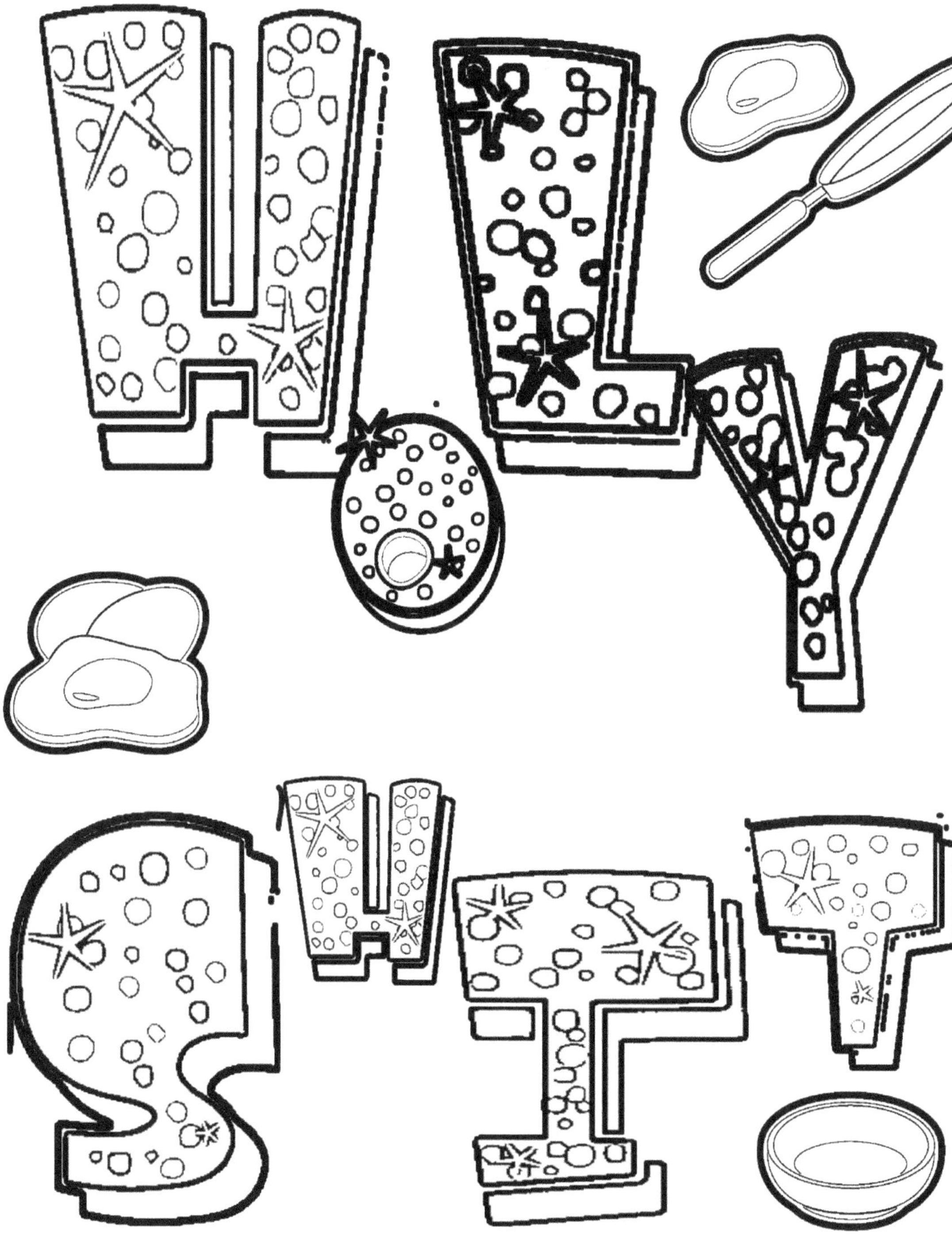
HOLY
SHIT!

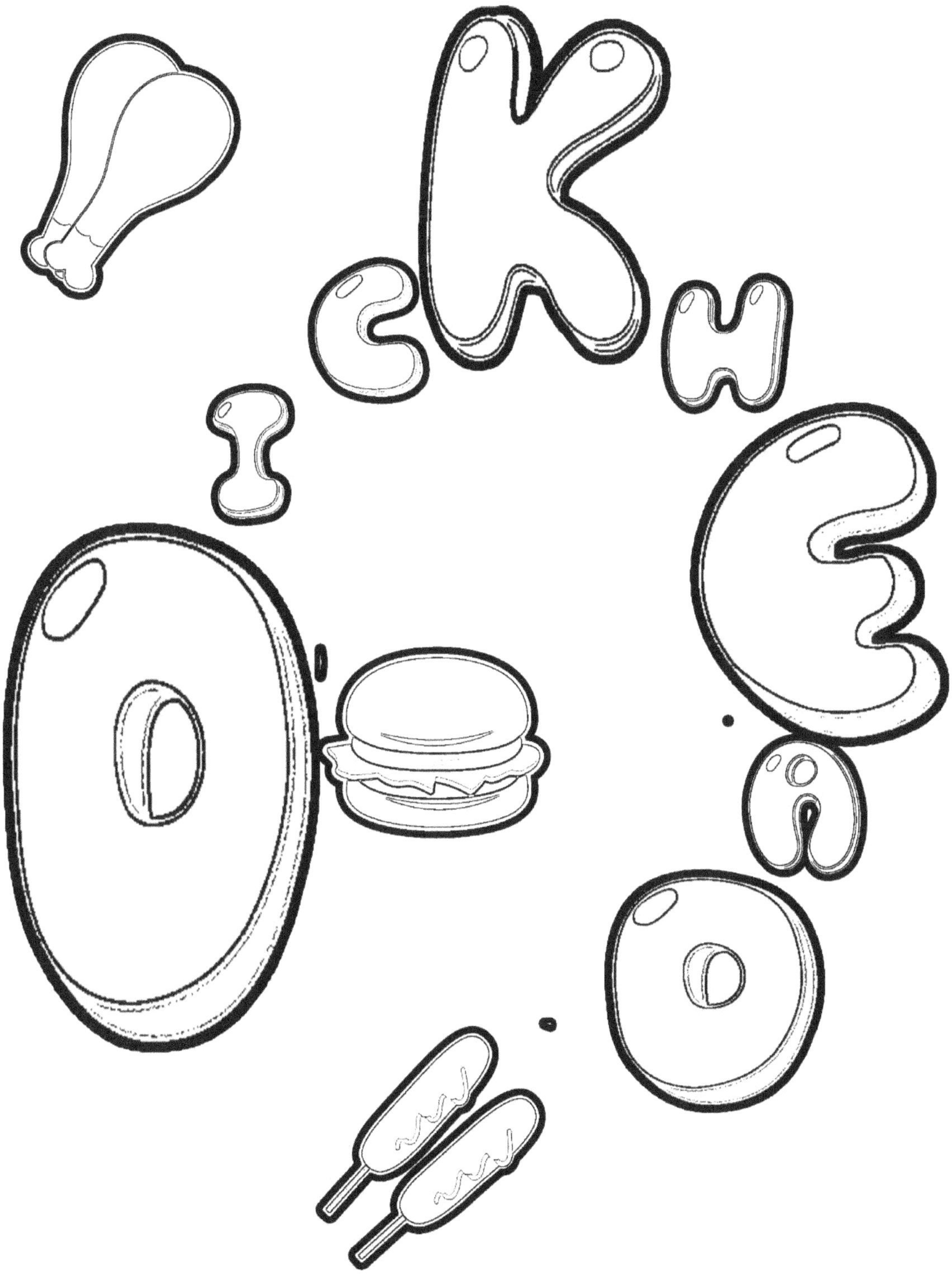

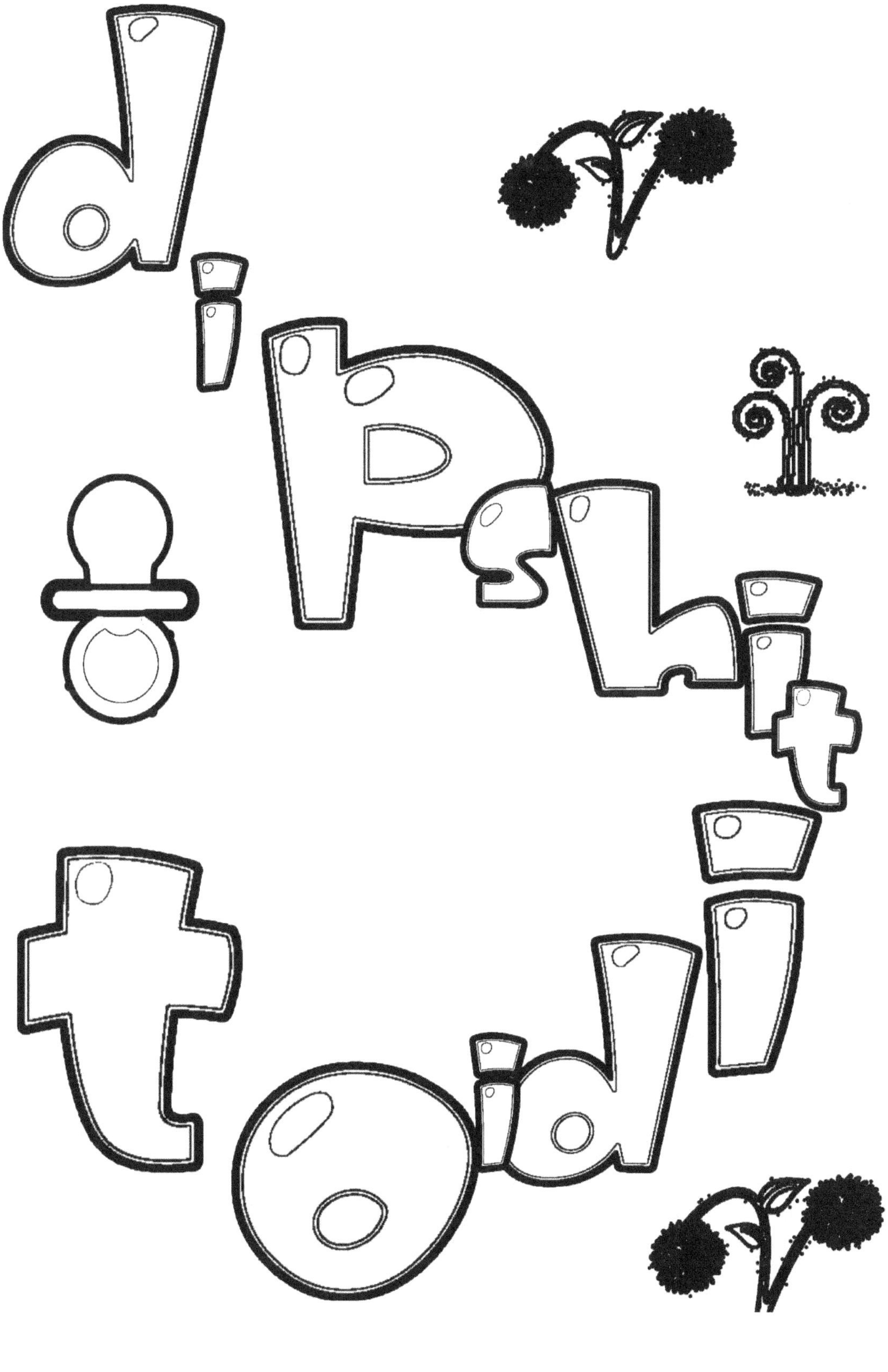
dipshit
idiot

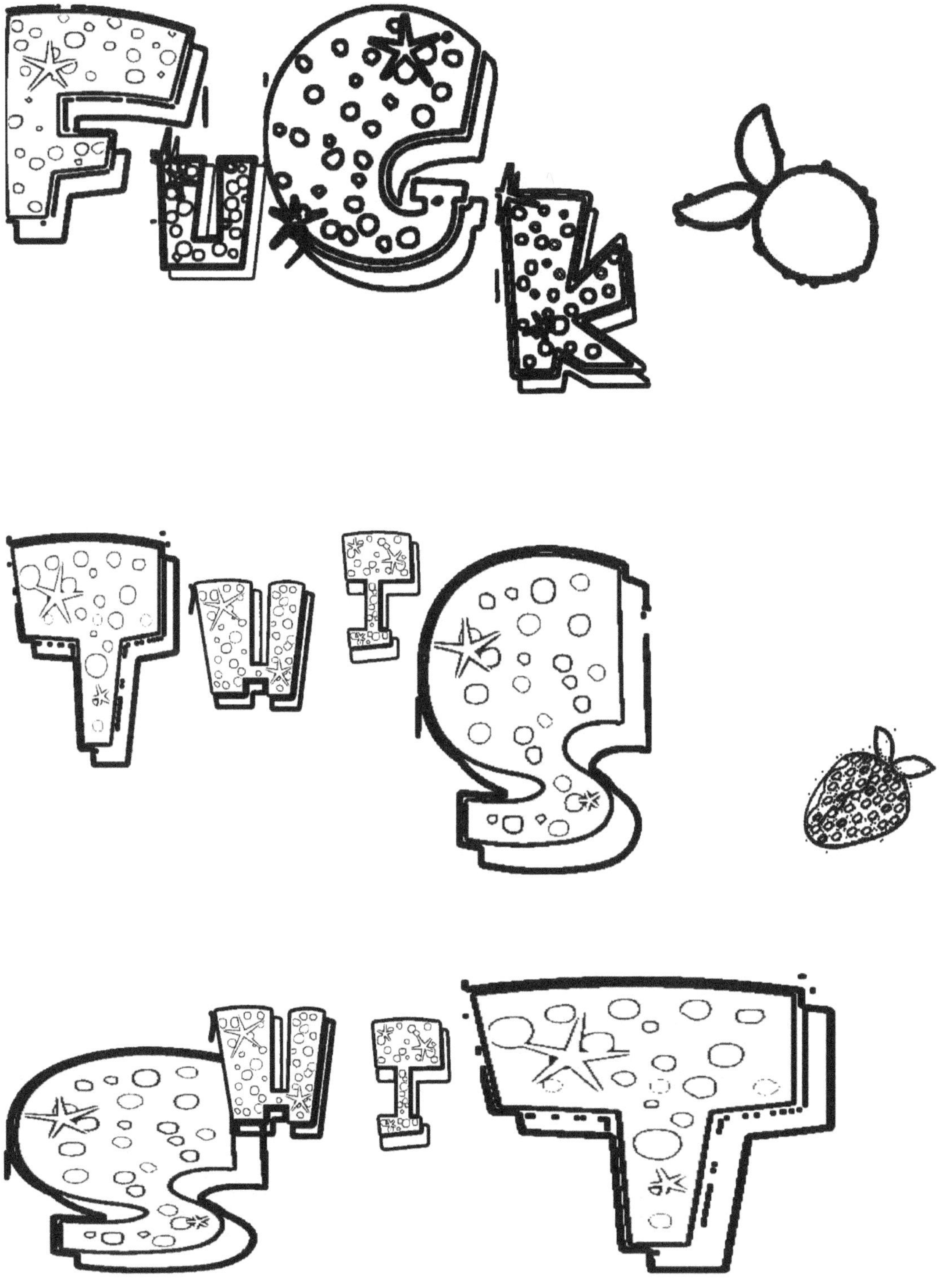
FUCK
THIS
SHIT

Note

www.ingramcontent.com/pod-product-compliance
Lightning Source LLC
Chambersburg PA
CBHW080641190526
45169CB00009B/3458
9781530999675